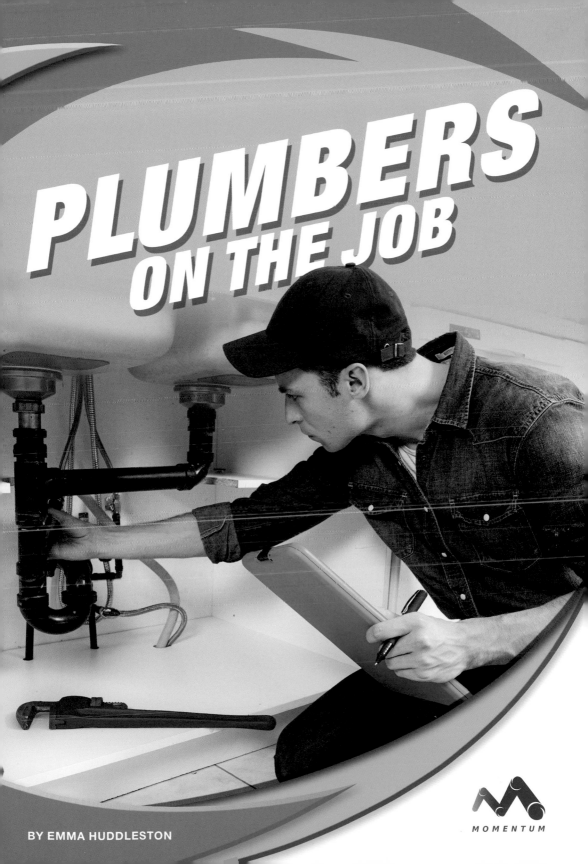

PLUMBERS
ON THE JOB

BY EMMA HUDDLESTON

MOMENTUM

Published by The Child's World®
1980 Lookout Drive • Mankato, MN 56003-1705
800-599-READ • www.childsworld.com

Content Consultant: Steven M. Gilmore,
Master Plumber, Instructor, St. Cloud Technical
and Community College

Photographs ©: Shutterstock Images, cover,
1, 11, 18, 28; iStockphoto, 5, 6, 15, 16, 22, 27;
Billion Photos/Shutterstock Images, 8; Mega
Pixel/Shutterstock Images, 9; Jo Ann Snover/
Shutterstock Images, 12, 14; John Vlahidis/
iStockphoto, 20; Denis Klimov 3000/Shutterstock
Images, 23; Monkey Business Images/
iStockphoto, 24

ISBN 9781503835504
LCCN 2019943072

Printed in the United States of America

CONTENTS

MOMENTUM

FAST FACTS

What's the Job?

► Plumbers **install** and repair pipes. They also install things such as bathtubs, sinks, toilets, dishwashers, and washing machines.

► To become a plumber, people need a high school diploma and need to complete an **apprenticeship**. Plumbers work full time. They also work nights, weekends, and whenever there is an emergency.

Important Stats

► In 2018, around 438,070 people worked as a plumber, pipefitter, or steamfitter in the United States. Pipefitters place pipes that carry acids, chemicals, and gases. They mainly work in large buildings and factories. Steamfitters are specialized pipefitters that work with steam pipes.

► By 2026, the number of jobs for plumbers, pipefitters, and steamfitters is expected to grow 16 percent, or by an additional 75,200 jobs.

► In 2018, the average yearly pay for these positions was around $58,150.

**Pipes carry liquids and gases to and from ►
buildings. Different buildings with plumbing
include businesses, homes, and factories.**

CHAPTER ONE

BECOMING A PLUMBER

Meg woke up earlier than usual. Today was her high school graduation. She put on a blue gown. It was her school's color. The blue graduation cap fit snugly on her head, and the gold tassel hung down by her cheek. When Meg walked across the stage, she heard the crowd clapping. All of her hard work in school paid off.

Dozens of blue caps flew into the air after the ceremony. Meg and her classmates threw them to celebrate. Then, her father rushed over, gave her a big hug, and handed her a silver-colored wrench. Meg smiled. The wrench was for her first day of work. Her dad was a plumber. That summer, Meg was going to start an apprenticeship with him.

On her first day, the wrench was heavy in Meg's hand. She put it in her dad's toolbox. They got into his truck and drove away.

◄ **Plumbers install boilers, which heat water.**

▲ **Plumbers use many different tools to get the job done.**

During her apprenticeship, Meg went with her dad to jobs. They fixed leaky toilets and sinks. One day, they helped a woman find her ring in a drain. She began her apprenticeship making about one-half of what fully-trained plumbers make. Her pay went up as she learned to do more. Meg met other people who had gone to school for a couple of years to become a plumber. In school, they took math classes and courses on how to repair and maintain pipes, how to read blueprints, and much more. Then, they got apprenticeships.

Meg's dad introduced her to clients. Being able to work with other people is one quality that plumbers need. Some jobs require a team of plumbers. They discuss the projects together.

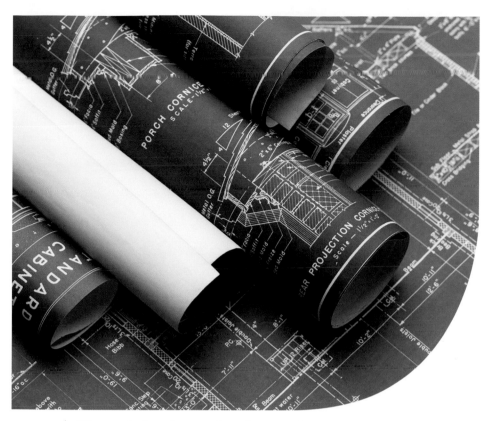

▲ **Blueprints show plumbers where pipes are or where they should be placed.**

Meg had the chance to learn from other experienced plumbers in addition to her dad.

One morning, Meg waved goodbye to her father. He was going to a plumbing job across town and she was going to a class. Meg took several classes during her apprenticeship. The company her father worked for offered them. She learned about safety, building **codes**, and how to read blueprints. Building codes come from the state. Some cities have more specific local rules. Blueprints are design sketches of buildings.

They show the layouts of rooms and walls. The paper has a grid printed on the background. This helps measure the size of each object, such as sinks.

Meg was an apprentice for a few years. She got around 7,000 hours of on-the-job training with her dad and learned a lot. Meg took a test to get her **license**. She proved her knowledge of the plumbing trade. Most states require plumbers to be licensed. They must pass an exam. They must also have two to five years of work experience.

Meg and her dad celebrated the end of her apprenticeship by getting ice cream. Meg was a **journey worker** plumber now. She was fully trained and could work on her own. She got hired at the same company as her dad.

On her first day of work as a journey worker, Meg's dad surprised her with a gift. It was a red toolbox. She took the bow off the shiny metal box and opened it. Her lucky wrench was inside. Meg picked it up and smiled. It had scratches and a few small dents. She used it almost every day. It had traveled with her to many jobs during her apprenticeship. Now, she would use it as she worked all on her own.

Apprentices learn a lot while working on the job. ►

CHAPTER TWO

HOUSE UNDER CONSTRUCTION

Through the dining room window, Mike could hear birds chirping outside. He flipped through his calendar to see how many tasks needed to get done that week. Mike was working on two plumbing jobs. One job was at a large factory. He worked with a crew there. In factories, steam can be used to make electricity that powers large machines. But the plumbing systems are complicated. They use huge steel pipes. It takes a crew and big equipment to keep such systems running. This week, the crew was scheduled to repair a large pipe.

At Mike's second job, he was installing plumbing for a house. The pipes were made of copper, steel, and plastic materials. Copper is the most common pipe material and has been used for centuries.

◄ **Plumbers need to follow certain codes when installing plumbing in homes.**

▲ **Pipes made out of different materials can be connected together.**

Before working on the house, Mike read the construction blueprints. He planned where the pipes would connect from room to room. He looked at the state and local building codes. Then, Mike gathered his tools. They included strong nails, a hammer, and a tape measure.

Mike drove to work. He walked through the house. His heavy work boots echoed loudly on the unfinished floors. Pieces of wood stood where the walls would be. Houses under construction were messy. Mike liked seeing them get completed over time.

▲ **Contractors need to work together to get projects done.**

The electrician was also at the house. He nodded at Mike to say hello. He and Mike were **contractors**. They helped build the systems that made the house work. The wires and pipes couldn't overlap. After Mike and the electrician finished their jobs, the walls and floors could be completed.

Mike made marks on the floors and walls. They showed where the gas lines and sewer lines would go. The house needed plumbing in many rooms. The bathroom had a toilet, sink, and bathtub. The basement had a water heater. It heated water to be used throughout the house. The kitchen had a sink and dishwasher.

For two weeks, Mike worked on the house. When he walked out for the last time, he saw the family's car pull into the driveway. He waved as he drove away.

CHAPTER THREE

SUDDEN LEAK

Pete woke up from the sound of his phone ringing. It was Saturday morning, and sunlight peeked through the window blinds. Pete grabbed his phone and saw that he was getting a work call. A client, Trevor, needed Pete's help. His bathtub had a leak, and Pete was a plumber. Plumbers have to be ready to work in emergencies, even on weekends. Pete got ready, grabbed his toolbox, and drove off in his truck.

Trevor looked relieved when Pete arrived. He showed Pete the brown spot on the ceiling where water had leaked. It was slowly dripping down into a bucket that Trevor had put on the floor. Then, they walked upstairs to the bathroom. Pete thought the problem could be with the drain pipes. Those pipes drain water from the tub to the city sewer system in the street. Pete needed to **inspect** the pipes.

◀ **Rusty and old pipes can spring leaks.**

▲ **Water leaks can cause a lot of damage to a house.**

The tub was fit tightly between two walls in the bathroom. The drain pipes were located near the base of the tub. If Pete cut into the wall in the bathroom, he would only see the top half of the pipes. Luckily, the tub was connected to a closet in the next room. Pete cut a hole in that wall. He used a flashlight to look at the pipes. He located the **drain trap**. It was a U-shaped pipe.

Sinks, toilets, and tubs all have drain traps. Their shape keeps a small amount of water in the bottom. This prevents gas and sewer smells from coming back up the drain and into the house. Pete followed the drain pipes. He found a loose fitting. Fittings connect pipes. They come in different shapes and sizes.

Pete repaired and tightened the fitting. This stopped the leak. He tested the rest of the pipe system to make sure it was working properly. He turned the bathtub on. He watched for leaks. Then he touched the pipes to see if he felt any water. The system was fixed.

During the repair, Pete noticed the pipes were old. They were worn down from use. It happens to all metal pipes over time. Water pushes forcefully through the small openings. This causes them to **corrode**. Worn-down pipes could cause a bigger problem for Trevor in the future. Pete suggested that he replace them. He prepared cost estimates for Trevor. He helped him choose the best option. Trevor considered different pipe materials. Some are more expensive than others, but they last longer.

Trevor thanked Pete for his advice. He also thanked him for helping out on the weekend. Plumbers can work odd hours. Multiple jobs might be scheduled for the same day. Plumbers also deal with a variety of work environments.

CHAPTER FOUR

DANGEROUS JOB

Eli got out of bed and stretched. His back was sore. Yesterday, he had bent over and reached into tight spaces in someone's basement. His wife shook her head. She thought Eli should **retire** soon. Many plumbers and trade-job workers were expected to retire by 2026. That makes trade-job workers in high demand. Young people need to replace the number of people retiring from the workforce.

The smell of bacon and eggs filled the kitchen. Eli finished breakfast. Then, he drove to work. As soon as he arrived, someone named Molly called. Her stove was leaking gas. Gas leaks can be really dangerous. They let harmful chemicals into the air, and it's not good to breathe them. Gas leaks can also cause an explosion. The gas can make people feel sick and tired. It can kill people if they are around the gas for too long.

◄ **Plumbers can be exposed to many dangers, such as close contact with mold.**

▲ **Natural gas explosions can damage buildings and kill people.**

Eli told her to leave her house and call the gas company to turn off the gas.

As soon as Eli arrived, he got to work. He found that some pipe fittings were bad and needed to be replaced. He fixed everything and called Molly. He told her it was safe to come back home.

Plumbers work in many situations and it can be a dangerous job. Tight work spaces can lead to injuries. Climbing ladders and working in construction sites can be risky. Most of all, exposure to **hazardous** materials is dangerous. Hot water, mold, and bacteria are common in water and sewage systems.

**▲ Plumbers don't always know what
they will find inside pipes.**

Some cleaning liquids and gases have harmful chemicals
in them. They can spark a fire. They can also cause health
problems if they get into someone's body.

When Eli got home that night, he made dinner. Eli and his wife
ate at the table as the sun set outside. Eli knew he would retire
eventually, but not yet. Plumbing jobs are in demand. Not only are
they needed for new construction jobs, but plumbers are needed
to repair and maintain existing plumbing systems. Some older
buildings and pipes need to be updated to follow state codes.
Eli had plenty of work to do.

CHAPTER FIVE

FAMILY BUSINESS

K evin drove his kids to the big brick high school. He dropped them off and waved goodbye. It was career day, and Kevin hoped they learned about a variety of career paths. Sometimes schools offer college as the best option for everyone. But Kevin knew college wasn't the only path to success. He was a plumber. He had taken over his dad's family business ten years ago. But he started working with his dad several years before that.

Kevin went to a local coffee shop to read the newspaper. He had a little extra time before his first job. It was nice to be an independent contractor. Independent contractors can work for themselves or for a business. They are hired and paid to do a certain task. This means their work varies. Kevin was enjoying a slow week after a hectic workload the week before. He worked more than 40 hours and he did several jobs.

◀ **Students can take plumbing classes to learn more about the trade.**

A contractor's work can be flexible. It depends on when clients need plumbing done.

Mrs. Monroe was Kevin's first client this week. She was 80 years old. Kevin's father had been her plumber many years ago. She greeted Kevin with a smile. She asked him to do a simple repair on a sink, which was leaking a bit. Kevin grabbed a hand auger. It was a tool used to unclog pipes. He pushed the long skinny metal tool down the drain. It had a coil at the end, which caught hair or other common clogs and pulled them out. Plumbers have to own the proper equipment if they want to have their own business.

When Kevin picked his kids up from school, he turned down the volume of the radio. They started talking about career day. They were interested in continuing the family business. Kevin thought they would be great at the trade. His kids were good at math. They also liked the challenge of solving problems. Plumbers solve problems for many kinds of situations, and they always have to think on their feet. They can also specialize in the field. For example, sprinkler fitters are experts with fire sprinkler systems. Steamfitters work with different water systems. Kevin knew several specialized plumbers.

They arrived at home. Everyone sat in the living room to relax. His kids wanted to learn more about the trade.

▲ **Pipes can become clogged with
things such as hair and dirt.**

Kevin explained that he was a master plumber. Master plumbers
take a test to prove their advanced skill and knowledge.
Some plumbers want additional training to prepare them to
supervise journey workers and to train apprentices.

▲ **Plumbing is important for everyday life.**

Additionally, master plumbers have a minimum of one year of experience as a journey worker. Most have more than five years of experience. This gives them time to find clients, too. Kevin felt lucky. He was able to immediately use the clients his dad worked with, such as Mrs. Monroe. The kids smiled. They knew her. She brought cookies over at least once every winter.

Suddenly, Kevin's phone rang. He answered and heard his neighbor's familiar voice. She had put potato peels down her drain disposal, and now the disposal was jammed. Kevin told her he would come over. After he hung up, he laughed to himself.

People will always need a plumber's skills to fix problems big and small. He invited his kids to come along.

Plumbing is part of daily life. It makes people's lives more comfortable, and plumbers are important in keeping systems working smoothly. They are needed in every state and at every time of year.

THINK ABOUT IT

▶ What is one part of a plumber's job that you already knew about? What is one piece of new information that you learned about plumbers?

▶ If you were a plumber, would you be more interested in working in small buildings such as homes or large buildings such as factories? Explain your answer.

▶ Why is it important that young people go into trade jobs to replace people who are retiring?

▶ What would your everyday life look like without plumbing?

GLOSSARY

apprenticeship (uh-PREN-tis-ship): An apprenticeship is a type of supervised work where someone learns trade skills. To become a plumber, a person needs to complete an apprenticeship.

codes (KOHDZ): Codes are rules or instructions. Plumbers have to learn about building codes.

contractors (KAHN-trak-turz): Contractors are people who work based on a contract for a specific task or job. People hire contractors when building a house.

corrode (kuh-RODE): To corrode is to break away little by little. Metal can corrode over time from contact with air or water.

drain trap (DRAYN TRAP): A drain trap prevents sewer smells from coming up through the pipe. The plumber looked at the drain trap to make sure it was working properly.

hazardous (HAZ-ur-duhs): A hazardous material can cause harm. Some gases are hazardous because they can catch on fire.

inspect (in-SPEKT): To inspect is to look closely at something. Plumbers inspect pipes.

install (in-STAWL): Install means to put in or set up a new system. Plumbers install pipe systems.

journey worker (JUR-nee WUR-kur): A journey worker is a person who has learned a trade and is an experienced worker. Meg worked hard to become a journey worker.

license (LYE-suhns): A license is a document that allows a business or person to perform work. She got her license to be a plumber.

retire (re-TIRE): To retire is to stop working full time. Many people retire when they are more than 60 years old.

TO LEARN MORE

BOOKS

Freedman, Jeri. *Plumber.* New York, NY: Cavendish Square, 2016.

Kamberg, Mary-Lane. *A Career as a Plumber, Pipefitter, or Steamfitter.* New York, NY: Rosen Publishing, 2018.

Roza, Greg. *How Do Sewers Work?* New York, NY: PowerKids Press, 2017.

WEBSITES

Visit our website for links about plumbing: **childsworld.com/links**

Note to Parents, Teachers, and Librarians: We routinely verify our Web links to make sure they are safe and active sites. So encourage your readers to check them out!

SELECTED BIBLIOGRAPHY

"Fix a Leak Week." *EPA*, n.d., epa.gov. Accessed 7 Mar. 2019.

Pamela M. "How to Fix a Leaking Bathtub." *Spruce*, 31 Jan. 2019, thespruce.com. Accessed 7 Mar. 2019.

"Plumbers, Pipefitters, and Steamfitters." *Bureau of Labor Statistics*, n.d., bls.gov. Accessed 7 Mar. 2019.

INDEX

ABOUT THE AUTHOR

Emma Huddleston lives in Minnesota with her husband. She enjoys writing children's books, but she likes reading novels even more. When she is not writing or reading, she likes to stay active by running, hiking, or swing dancing.